the **Light**
and
Dark pieces

Monique West

Contents

1. Light .... Page 1

2. Dark .... Page 56

3. Bonus .... Page 112

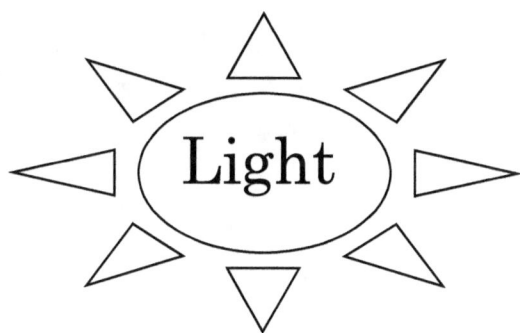

Don't doubt yourself

You're too unique to be following others, you're too special to not know your self-worth.

You see, beauty is way more than your appearance, beauty runs skin deep beauty is caring about someone who doesn't even care for themselves, beauty is bettering yourself so you can help and nourish the people around you;

Beauty is giving that smile to someone who's having a bad day, because as we age our physical beauty fades, but our inner beauty will forever stay the same.

The journey to somewhere is never easy

I'm walking blind folded not knowing where I'm going but know where I want to go with no idea how I'm going to get there, I'm walking blind folded and I trip and stumble a thousand times and each time it gets harder to get back up, but with hope and faith and knowing in my heart I'm destined to shine; I get myself up and force out a smile and carry on living my life.

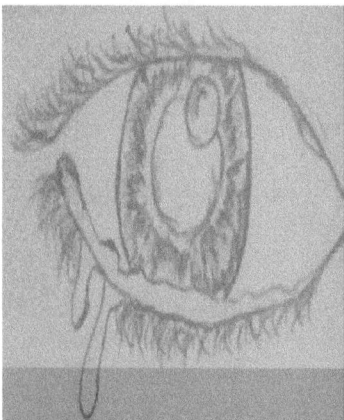

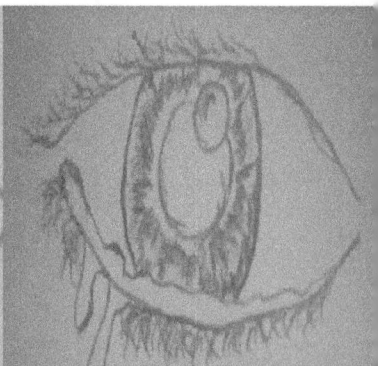

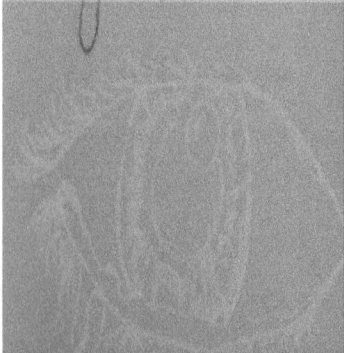

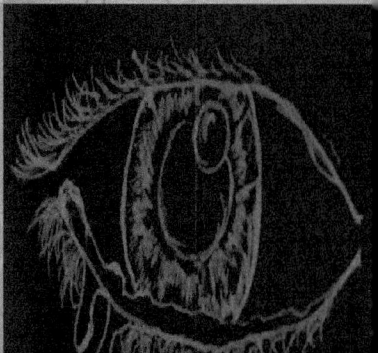

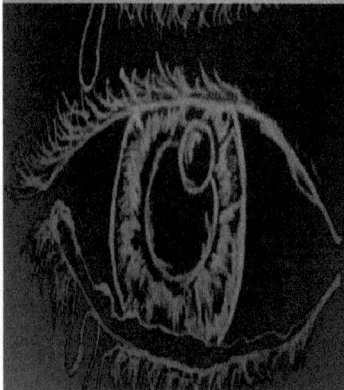

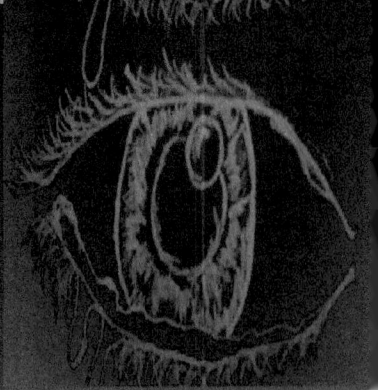

Don't know what to believe

My emotions run deep, when I feel for you, I feel for me. I'm disconnected from the world and that's how I like to be, I like to be alone, but I don't like to be lonely were all human beings but still we hate one another, betray one another mislead each other into destruction of our hearts and feelings. We say sorry but really do we mean it; were telepathically liars and we don't even see it.

Stop lying to yourself

The tears in your eyes make me think twice, I wonder if the life your living is really worth your life, you see I can see through the persona you paint to hide your pain, the persona you paint to distract you from a life your living which you hate.

You picture yourself somewhere you can escape, be yourself and show the real you; You want to be seen, not for who you are but who you want to be, So you lay in your bed silently and you dream of all you want and all you seek to be. Hoping that someday you'll live the life of which You seek.

Someone special

When I'm with you it's like I've
never experienced love before but
experiencing it for the first time.

You're a gift from the heavens,
something I never knew I needed,
you showed me how to have love
for life and for that i am conceded.

Lying to myself

You tell me all the things I want to
hear; you lie to me but really do I
care? I want to be loved so I'll
accept the worst.

Rather play dumb

You lie to me but really, I
know the truth; you lie to
my face and think I'm
oblivious to the lies your
telling. Yet I act a fool
waiting for the chance to
expose the truth.

Misunderstanding

Your face is something I
can't erase; I see you in my
dreams at night, wishing you
would go away.

It's not that I don't love you
but it's that I need to move
on and being stuck in a place
I can't move forward is killing
me, mentally and physically.

Don't wait

I want to be great, but greatness
seems too far away to be reached, so
what's the point in trying... that's
what I use to tell myself before I tried.

Don't be scared

I stand by the glass and
stare into the distant, I
see your face in the glass
but to me your so
distant.

Is it me that you seek
or are you looking for
someone, I told you a
thousand time to leave,
but every time you
stayed and told me
please,
You needed me.

But to me I don't believe;
I don't trust what you say,
how can you love me
so bad then you chose
to stay away.

I needed you and you
pushed yourself away
and said it was faith.

When in fact you feared

commitment, scared
to love, scared to trust
anyone and even though it
hurts just know I'll always
be here to pull
you up.

Confidence

Confidence is not so much to
be gained but recaptured.

Nothing but a fool

I trusted you, and you tore my heart
out you showed me your true colours
but I refused to believe that your
heart was so dried out, Silly me to
believe that there's beauty in
everyone,

that I thought I could change you
and make you into that someone.

You see I mourned you for the longest
time wishing that you were mine, and
now that I have you, I see that your
nothing more than a curse to my life.

Pressure

Don't think too hard or your brain
Might pop like skittles, you might
Think that you're managing but really
You're out of your mental.

All lies

He can love you and break your heart
a thousand times, he can shatter your
Spirit and confuse your mind. And
come back to you to only feed you
lies, with a I love you which only
means goodbye.

Why are we all living this lie?

The world only sees what
they want to see, they
see the bad and exploit
it, they see the good and
disregard it;

They want us to live in
fear and believe that
there isn't hope for
humanity when in fact,

the good is overpowering
the evil, but we just don't
see it.

To everyone who thinks they know me

How are you to know
someone who doesn't
even know themselves,

someone who's lost and
doesn't know what
direction they're going

someone's who's walking
blindfolded and stepping
over broken glass but still
hides how they're feeling
because they don't trust
anyone to see their real
truth.

My own person

They don't tell us but it's
clear that our opinion
doesn't matter,

We're our own person our
own being, yet there are
laws telling us what we can
and cannot do with our
body...... make it make
sense.

I rather be secretive than too open

Being vulnerable is allowing
someone to see the deepest and
harshest parts of you the good
and the bad,

exposing yourself to judgement,
perception, and interpretation
about you.

Allowing someone to look at you
and either understand you or have
no idea what you're about and
why you are, who you are, even
with a spread sheet explaining
your emotions.

Our life isn't ours until we make it

Ever since the day I could walk I was told that education was everything and if you don't have education you don't have anything"

you see we were programmed from birth to live a stable life, a life which was made and structured out for us thousands of years ago.

So, when we are born straight away, we have a purpose and are told who to be

however, we make our own destiny.

...Continuing

It's too late for me to
break from out this box
to become unstable,

I'm too head deep
in the system to let go;
because if I do now,

I just might land on my
feet or I'll land on my
face, either way it's a risk
I'm not willing to take.

A teacher

Your someone who didn't
care so much for the
opinions, you lived your
best life and followed your
dreams;

you weren't the best, but
you tried and succeed;

you weren't the smartest,
but you're learned and
achieved.

You tried your best so what
will be will be.

Someone I wish I knew

You're someone I wish I knew, so
wise so knowledgeable so open to
experience, your wisdom spoke its
own language and sung its own song,
it danced through the night turning
everything to gold.

You're someone I wish I knew.

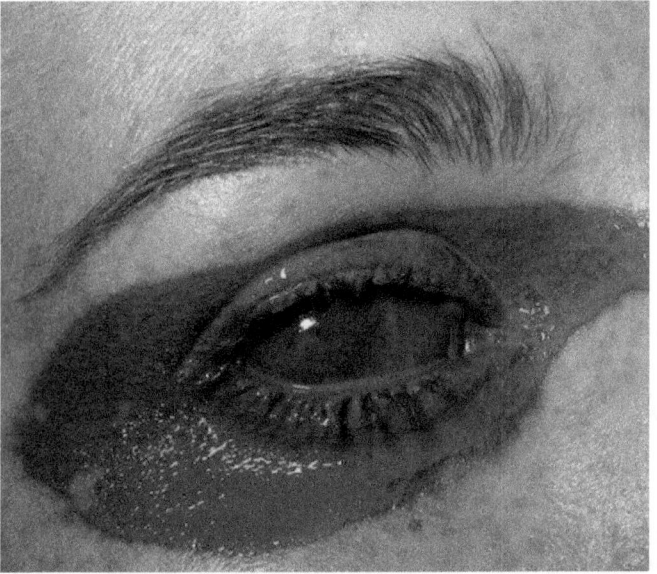

Don't want to know the truth

The pain in her eyes are real, all she wants is to be free, free to love, free to be herself and not worry about society judging her; she's so beautiful and she doesn't even know it, her hearts so pure yet all they see is her skin,

you see they judge for not what they know but what they see, and what they see is pure but their refusing to see.

Blinded by fake love

When I look at you, I feel your love, I
see your trust I see your encouragement
and I see your support, yet we don't see
eye to eye yet we argue about the little
things, and begin to drift away,

I love you, so it's hard for me
to see the truth, see that
your toxic for me and
I'm toxic for you.

I'm not good enough

Your love is like a tornado, it sucks me up and spits me out, but still I remain in the same place for you to come back and hurt me all over again,

I'm a fool what can I say.

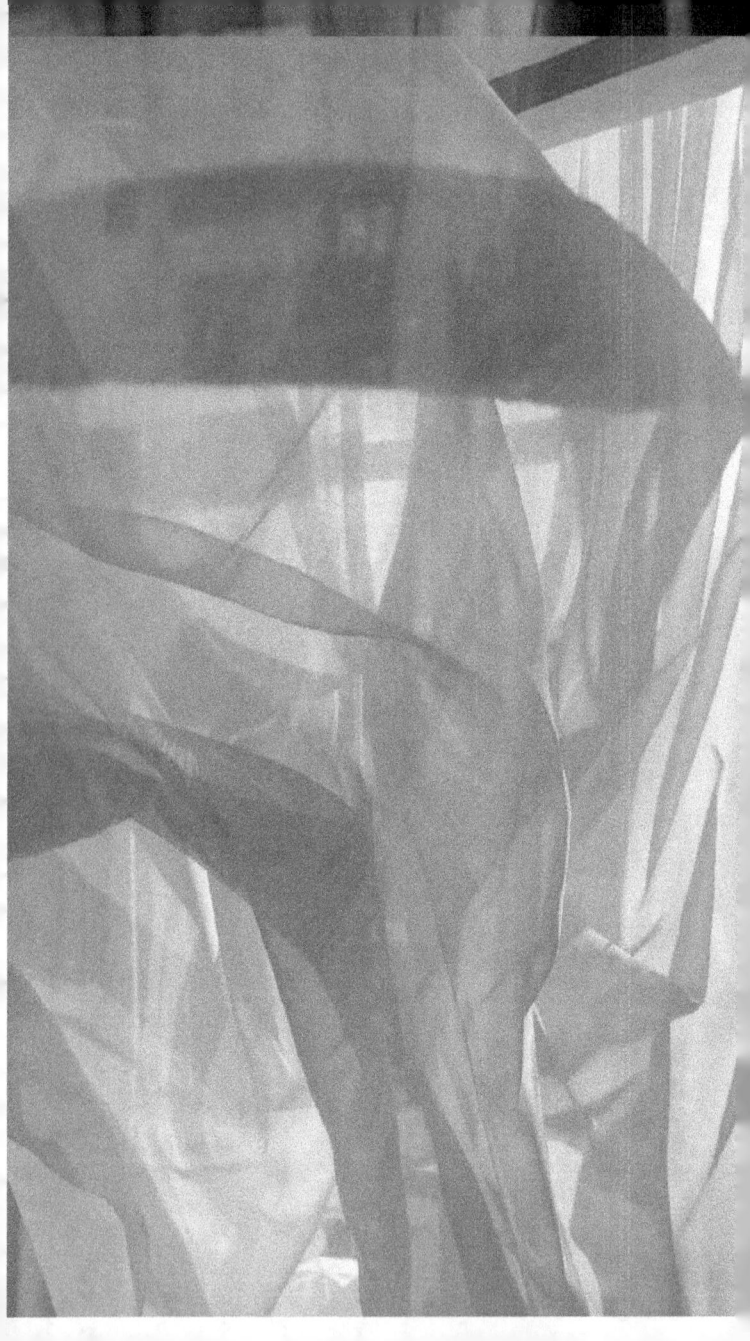

Watching from the side

It's summertime and the wind blows, you'll say it's hot, but I'll say it's cold, you'll say it's bright, but I'll say it's dark

Because this is how I feel,

my emotions are like the weather, I can't control it, it does what it does and does what it wants.

I want

I want to stare out in the sunset close
my eyes and feel all the negativity and
hurt release from my body;

I want to feel my soul cleanse as I rub
my hands into the sand and feel its
grainy texture as It drifts through the
palms of my fingers,

And on that day, I will be reborn into
someone who is even more beautiful,
caring, loving, and spiritual.

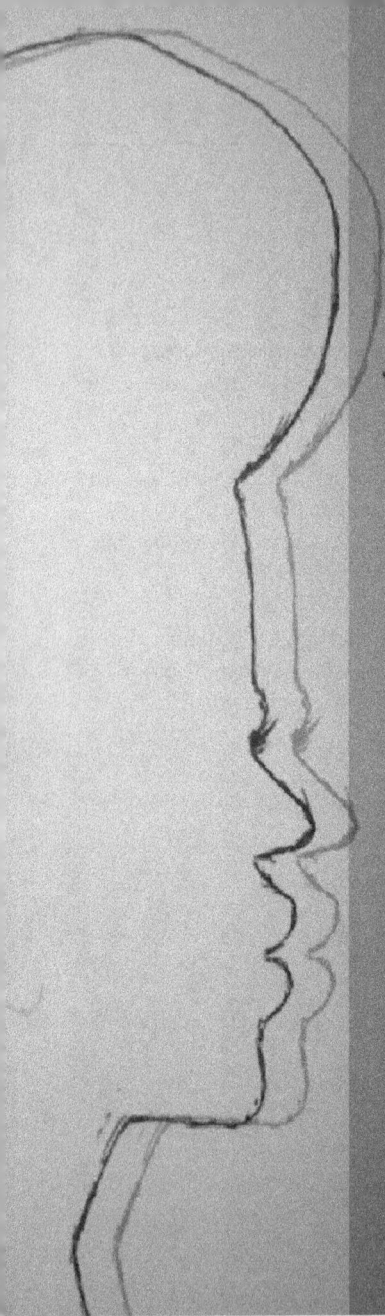

No thank you

Your pretty for a dark skin girl, is that
a compliment, are you waiting for a
thank you?

Because when you tell me that your
telling me that you hate dark skin
girls, but you'll make an exception for
me.

"Like I'm meant to be grateful"

Somewhere else

Right now, I'm somewhere
in my life where I feel as if
I'm stuck;

I'm on a train which keeps
getting delayed and keeps
making excuses for it being
delayed,

I'm somewhere in my life
where I need something
new, something exciting,
something exotic,
something that can stop my
thoughts from perceiving
me to want to fail.

If it isn't like this...then

You take me where I want
to be somewhere calm, still
and silent so I can hear the
bird's tweet.

It's like a dream when I'm
with you, nothing seems
real as if it's too perfect to
exist I'm not worth this
perfection, I'm not worth
being missed

but you showed me that I
am, he showed me that I'm
his.

No sympathy

She told me she loved me she
told me she cared but as soon as I
opened my heart, she closed hers
and she walked away, with no
hesitation she looked straight.

Guard to my heart

Your love is so pure your love is so
clear you brighten my spirit whenever
your near, you shelter my heart
protect me from pain you hold all the
keys, to unlock my chains.

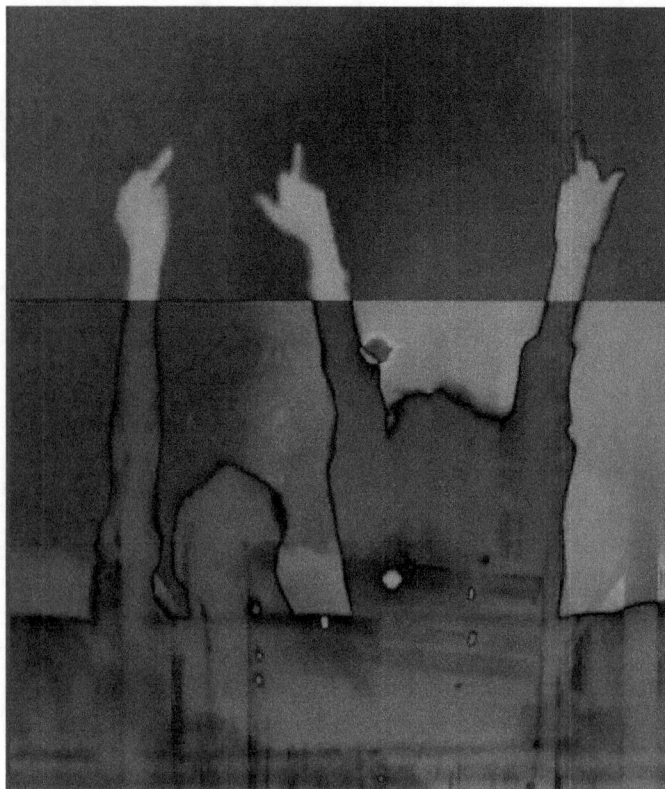

PERIODTTTT

No matter how hard you try you can never be perfect, no matter how hard you try to be liked not everyone will like you and that's okay,

because if your being you and being true to who you are who gives a shit what people think.

Find yourself and then stride

I'm sitting here staring at the
mountains, thinking about my
life and where I want to go,

and then I think to myself
wouldn't it be nice to be a
mountain, silence, peace, love,
beauty and free,

free from all the worries, free to
have time to get to know myself
"inside and out" and know the
true meaning of who I am.

Opposite

Why do you hurt so much why do you
feel so much pain, when you've done
nothing wrong, so innocent so sweet
but yet bad stuff happen to the
people who are most in need of
happiness.

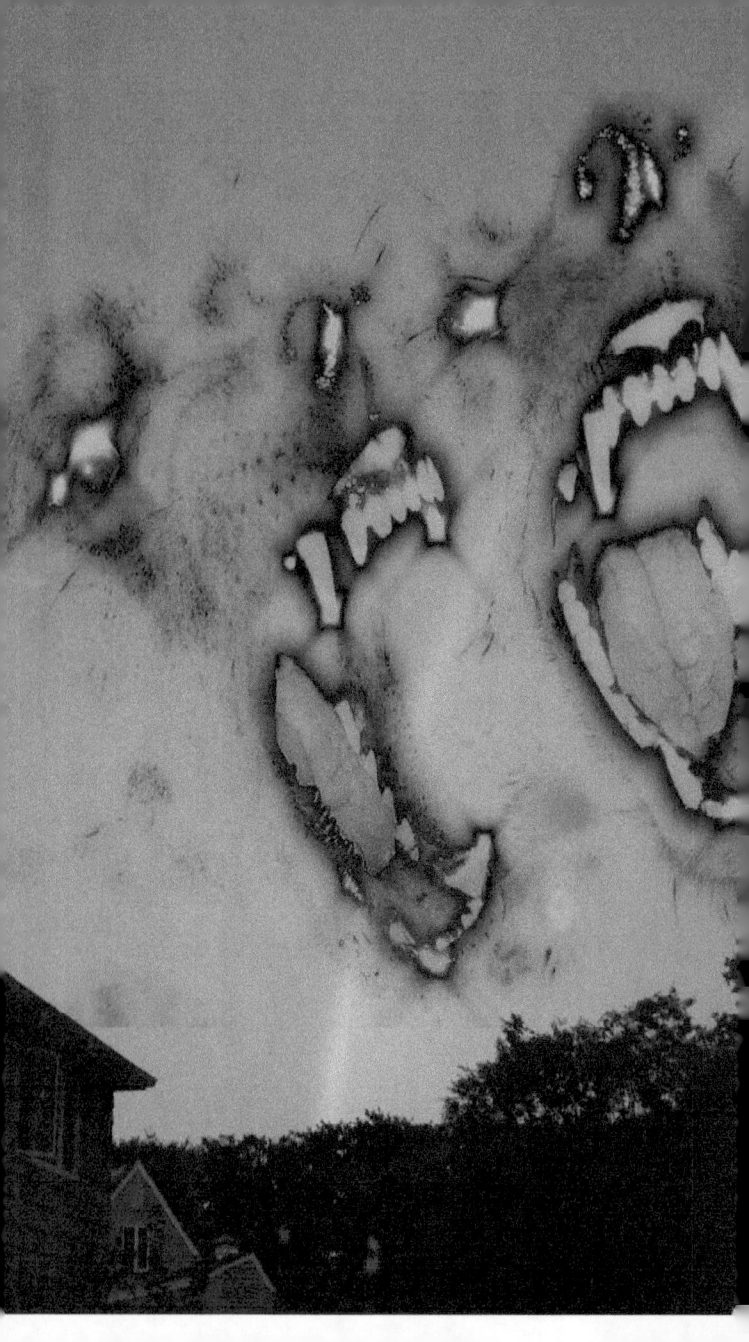

Wrong

We came on this earth with our bodies and souls. No objective shit, no money or phones no laws that objectify us to say we have to pay another human being to live in a home, no paying to eat or paying for water all stuff which should be free and a human right, just like my opinion.

This world was created to be free with love, not caged with hate.

What choice do I have?

My heart shines like a pendent,
my mind glistens like a chandelier,
to me your everything I wanted,
but to them your the venom in a
snake and when you kiss me, you
turn me dark, darker than the
gates of Hell,

you're like a drug that
I love but can kill me if I
take too much.

I don't want to leave,
I don't want to go,
but do I have a choice?
I would say no.

Now I don't want to hurt you
and I don't want to break
your heart, but your killing
me slowly and your killing
my heart.

Questions with no Answers

She knows exactly what she wants
but she just can't get it

the world is telling her no and forcing
her to let go, forcing her to choose
another path when all she wants is to
do that.

You see she wants the money she
needs it,

she can't be stuck in a job that works
her hard and pays her shit, because
she better than that.

She wants to succeed; she wants to
achieve but now that this path is
crumbling what is she to do now what
is she to believe.

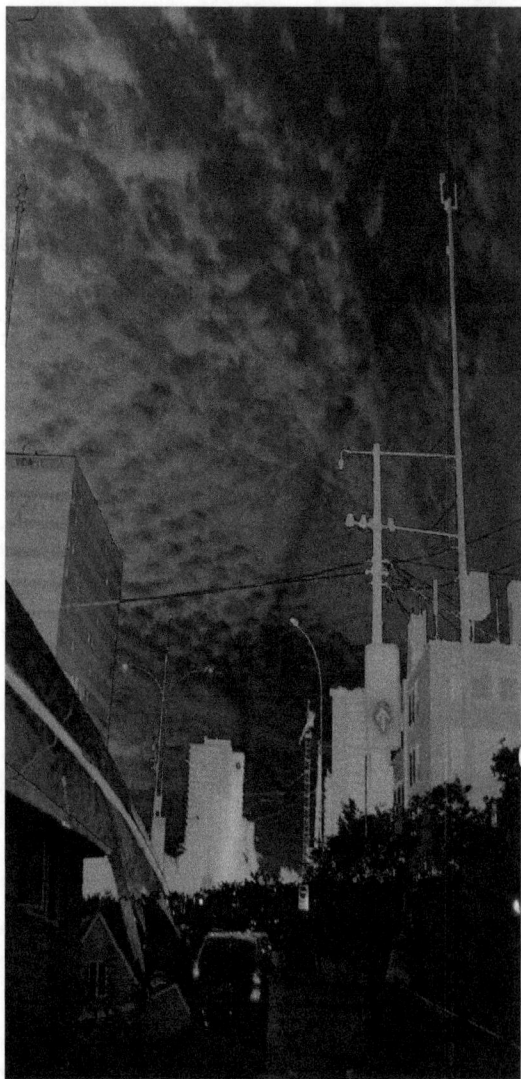

Never what you think

Today is never a reflection of
tomorrow, and tomorrow is never a
reflection of today. So, stop believing
that every day is going to be the
same, because there's always a little
change in every day...

As bodies and souls, we need to know
that everyday has a little change.

Imagine

Imagine living in a world where all
our essential needs were free, and
all opinions were valued as much
as the top mans.

Imagine a place where no judgement
was poured out upon someone
who was different, and everyone
accepted one another......imagine
a world.

Go through it to get through it

The pain you have to go through
Is sometimes necessary for you to
appreciate the small things.

Seeing my Self worth

Don't tell me you love me when all
you do is hurt me; don't tell me you
care when all you do is break my
heart. I'm done with all the sorry's I'm
done with all the no's, you're not
enough for me and it's okay for me to
let you go.

Good old days

Her voice was sweeter than a
bird's tweet in the morning,
sweeter than that one blueberry
which hides in the basket,

and when she sang the flowers
would blossom and the birds
would begin to chirp, I'd get
goosebumps up and down my
body from my head to my toes
and back up again

I've never heard a voice so
beautiful until I hear my
grandma sing.

Stop wasting your time

The love he's offering is useless,

you need more than I love you, sorry
and I'll never do it again (for the 4th
time) sorry;

Your better than this, and your too
good for him, and it's okay for you to
let yourself know that it's time for you
to go.

Alive

When she sang, she felt safe, free to
be herself, and free enough to expose
her vulnerability in her songs;

her emotions traveled through her
body and out her fingertips and into
the keys of the black and white piano,

I've never seen a piano so lonely and
a person so alive

the stage was her first home, and her
house was her second you see she
sang to make an impact a change in
our thoughts and our minds and when
we would listen our feelings would
mourn and we would feel alive.

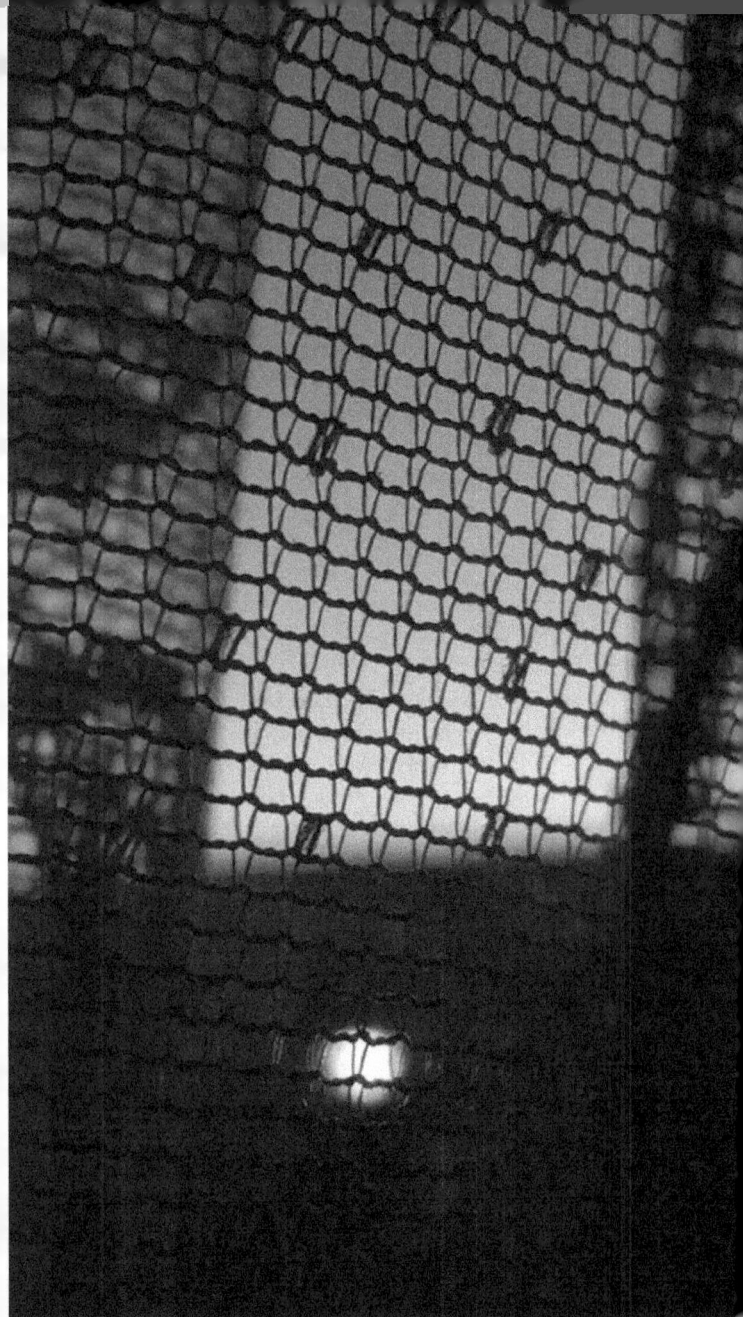

Why

While the sun shines in my face, I
close my eyes and try to think all that
is good in my life, But nothing seems
to come to mind; I slowly open my
eyes and glaze right into the sun and
think to myself the world is beautiful,
yet I live a life of pain. "Why"

Smile

A warm feeling inside of me I never
felt, I'm getting hugged from the
inside with a warm mushy felt.

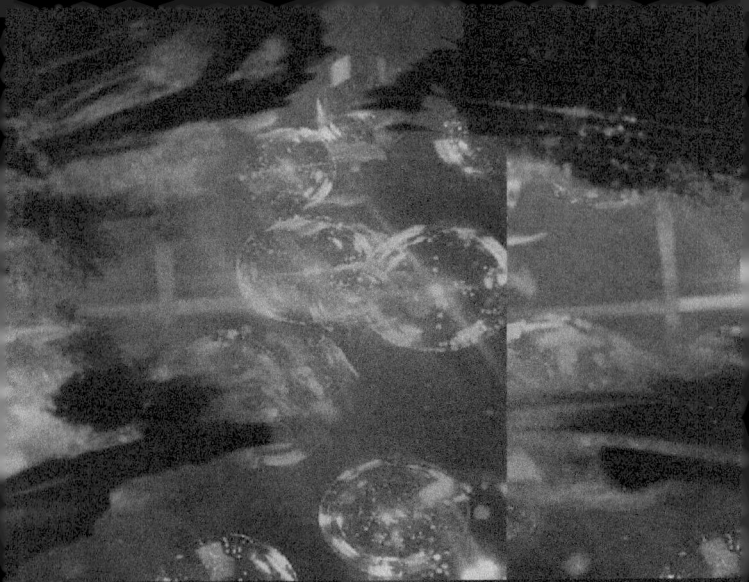

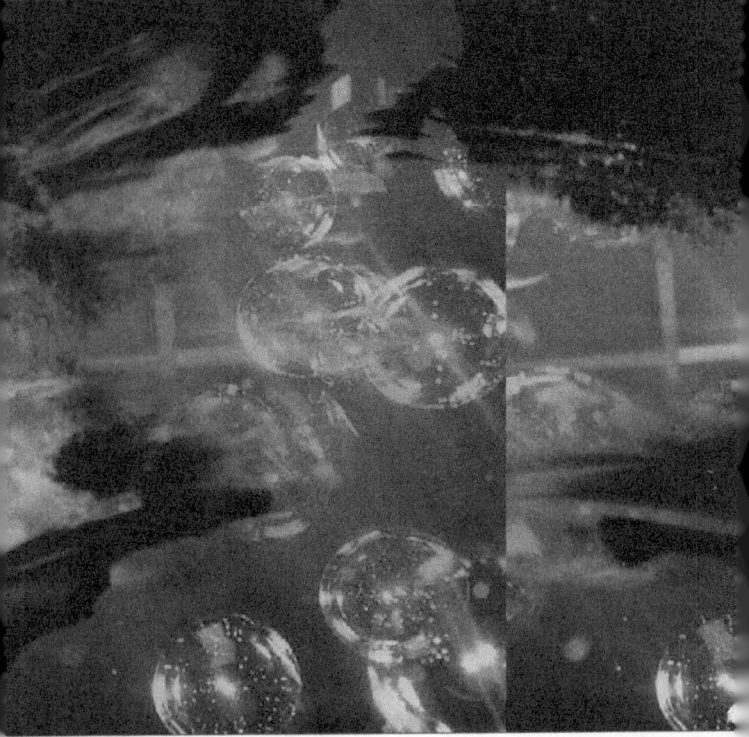

Gloryful

This feeling is more than a feeling it's
a touch an energy which is passing
through me from the universe,

It contains in my body and is growing
in my heart; I can feel its glory and
feel its love.

A forever feeling

I'll tell you how I'm feeling but it's
better for me to keep it inside, I
want it to consume me, nourish
me and forever make me feel
alive.

A new beginning

I'm glowing from the inside
and it's showing in my face,
it's a feeling I never felt
before, and a feeling I never
want to erase.

Kings and queens

They don't want us to be
great, their taking away our
prophets and our leaders
because their scared of our
evolution,

the knowledge we've
gained and the power we
have, they don't want us to
know that we're powerful,
we're strong and together
we can change everything,
but their trying to suppress
us from the truth;

We are worthy.

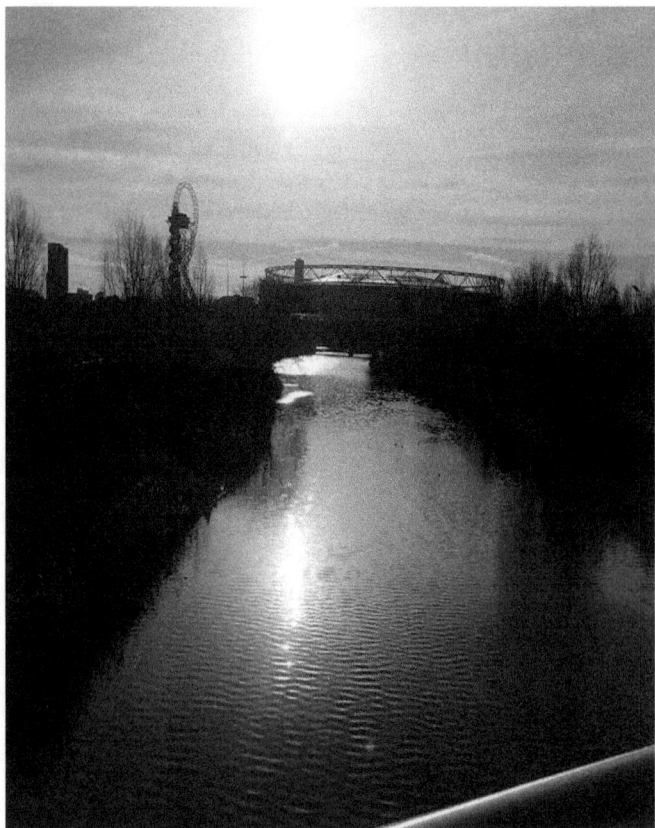

We're all someone

We all want to be someone but don't want to put in the work, we expect gifts to fall out of the sky and into our laps.

I know it's easier for some to succeed more than others but success is success and when you work hard it's guaranteed in some way or another.

I can't lie, but

The world would be so much calmer if
everyone cherished alone time, there
would be more success if we all stayed
in and focused on our passions and
worked on ourselves.

Now I'm not saying to be a loner nor
I'm saying to be lonely, I'm just saying
that success would be more likely if
you stayed in and worked on your
craft.

We gotta focus

We live our lives all wanting to be someone, having a passion but most with no drive to fulfil it, were all unique beings and are cable of anything we put our minds to, as long as we stay locked in and focus on what we want to be.

I want

I want to create a world where its sole
purpose is to look after the world and its
animals where trees grew where it wanted,
and animals weren't hunted, somewhere
where guns never existed and colour wasn't
an issue. Somewhere calm, peaceful and silent.

Dark

Living a dream

She's hurting so bad that she doesn't even see the real in reality she's lost in a world that isn't real and she's the only one alive but doubtfully unaware of her surroundings, she escapes but only for a period of time and is suck right back in. She figures this is the life she's just meant to have a life full of pain and hurt where nothing can cure it.

It's okay

Leave me lonely by myself,
all I want is the darkness
and shadows, I'm afraid of
the light because I'm afraid to
get hurt, so leave me lonely,
leave me be, and move on
without me because it's okay
for you to be free.

I'm hiding from myself

I'm cage in the darkest parts of my
mind, shut away from existence,
hidden from the light like a creature
in the night. I watch from the outside
looking in thinking why; What's the
purpose of life if all we seem to
endure is pain in Disguise.

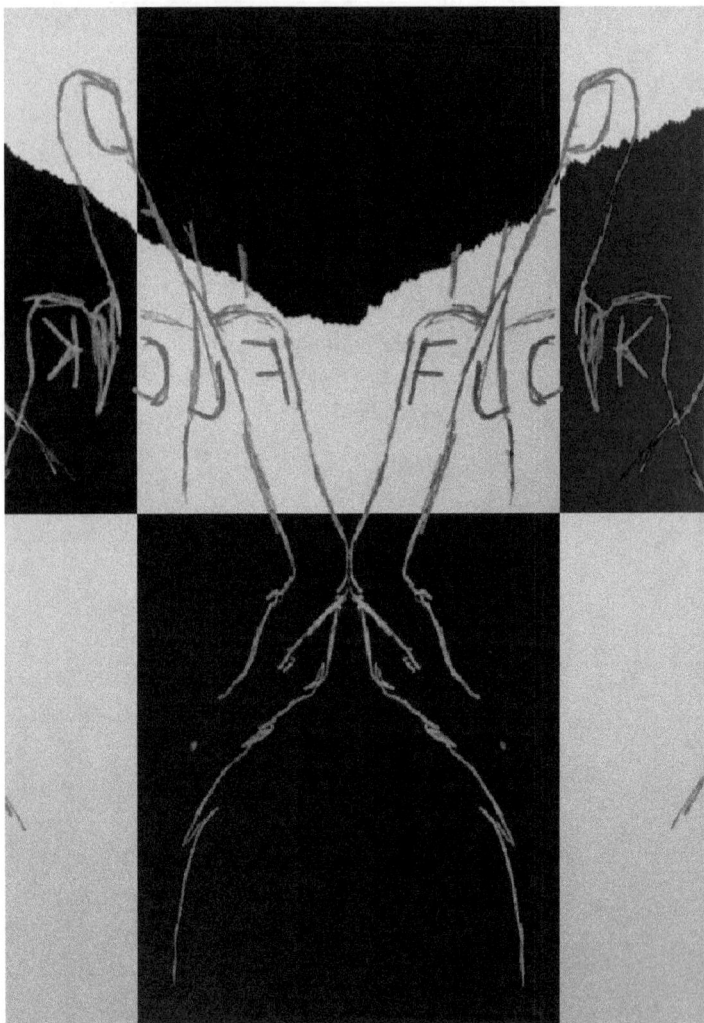

Mind fucked

It's not you that I hate it's my own -
self being, I'm a person who likes the
darkness but hates the trauma that
comes with it.

I never know

The darkest parts of me always seem to
become me in the worst times, like I'm
playing tag with who I'm going to be today,
like am I myself or the other person who
likes the dark and isolation as her friend.

What I'm choosing

I always seem to get stuck in positions
where I don't want to be, always
seem to get surrounded by people
who I hate to see,

who I don't hate necessarily but hate
socializing and acting friendly because
I know they're not the people for me.

Nowhere to run

I try to escape the dark cloud that
follows me but, it always seems to
catch up and swallows me again,
which puts me in a trans where
darkness is my keeper and I'm its
prisoner once again.

He said it.

Damn Is it too much to ask for, I'm ready to die, take me before I change my mind. I'm suffocating being eaten alive my body doesn't want me so it's dissolving my insides, a sense of nothingness I feel ring inside my body I'm lost in the dessert without water to help me heal the thirst inside.

Never in control

I close my eyes and all the
sounds are heightened,
suddenly everyday sounds
become irritating and I
begin to feel a pressure on
my chest,

slowly it becomes harder
and suffocation is what
I'm starting to feel,
you see I'm suffocating
not physically but
mentally, and I can't
seem to control it.

Too late?

I'm so fucking lost I feel I will never
find my way back; I'm so far gone I
feel there's no helping me,

I'm gone and I'm dead inside, I'm here
physically but really my spirit is dead
and there's no reviving me.

Alive

My eyes roll to the back
of my head, as I stare at
you, I feel I'm dead, my
heart stops for a minute
and I drift away into the
distance.

Suddenly I'm alive and
awake in a place which is
vibrant, with no sounds
but the Whistling sounds
of the wind gushing
against the leaves of the
trees.

I feel calm, radiant, a
spiritual being who has
just found herself.

Alone not lonely

As much as I hate being lonely, I love being alone, A sense of release and peace from the world, I sit alone in my room and gather myself for the days to come.

Your trying to figure it out

The life your living is full of anger
you walk around with torment on
your face and pain on your chest,
it's like a cold that doesn't go
away but sticks with you until it
chooses to leave by its self.

Realization is a bitch

I wake up and look at myself in the
mirror; damn I look like shit but it's a
good representation of how I'm
feeling, lost, confused and tired, tired
both physically and mentally it's
exhausting being depressed feeling
lost and confused all the damn time,
its fucking exhausting.

Darkness
awakes

As I walk through
the shadows of death,
I feel your stare burn
through my chest,
I drop unconscious
into the gates of Hell

and wake up in a place
which seems like death,
am I Alive or am I dead,

am I dreaming or is it all
in my head I don't know,
but all I know is that I'm
feeling killing, murderous,
horrendous pain.

Which is not physical but
mental, and even though
I feel I'm dead, I feel
like I'm dying all over
again, from the
inside out,

my body is eating me
alive and all I can do

is stare at the
devil's sky's and
ask God why.

Loneliness is sometimes the best cure

she wishes she could break out of this world
and go somewhere, where there were no
people no sign of life , she wishes she was free
to make her own destiny and free to express
her feeling and not worry about how people
would perceive her. She just wishes the world
was basic and not so much out of the ordinary.

Evolving

Because I'm me today doesn't mean I'll be me tomorrow, stop expecting me to stay the same when the world is always changing.

Pain is pain

I hold my heart in my hand and I
walk towards my pain wishing it
will go away, but it always seems
to stay and cause more pain.

Months off

I'm distance from myself, I'm here but
I'm not really here, I'm consciously
aware of my surroundings, but have
no intention in wanting to interact;

I want to be left alone, why is it so
hard for you to understand, give me a
couple weeks and I'll eventually get
back to who you want me to be.

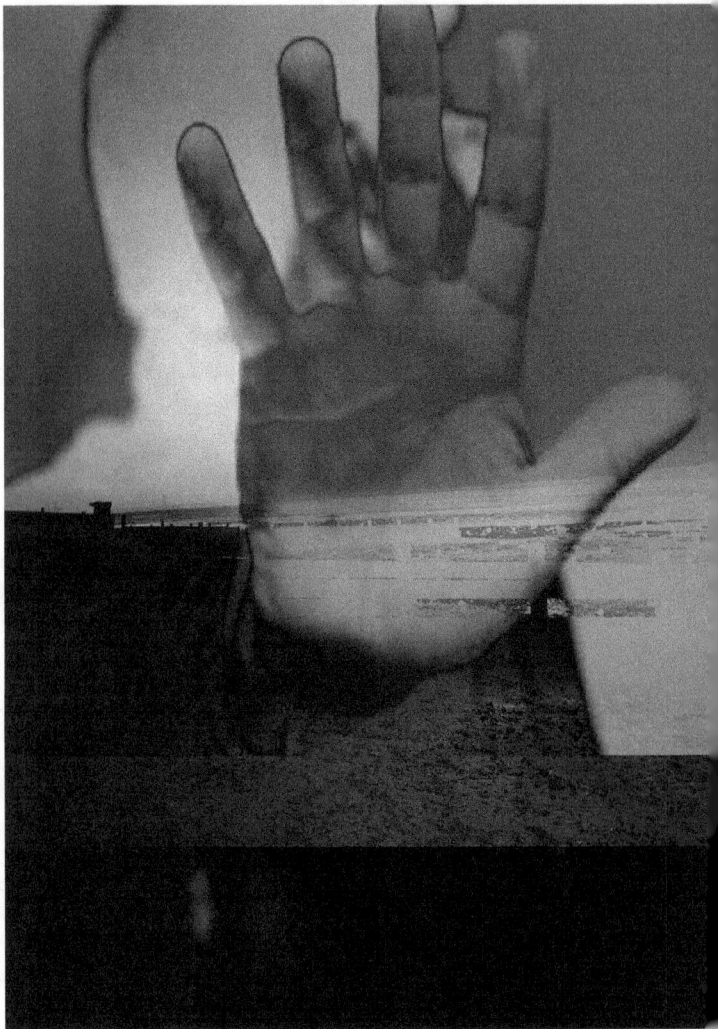

Deceiving myself

You told me the truth, but I refused to
believe you, it'll hurt too much if it
was true so I'll just deny, deny until I
can't deny the truth.

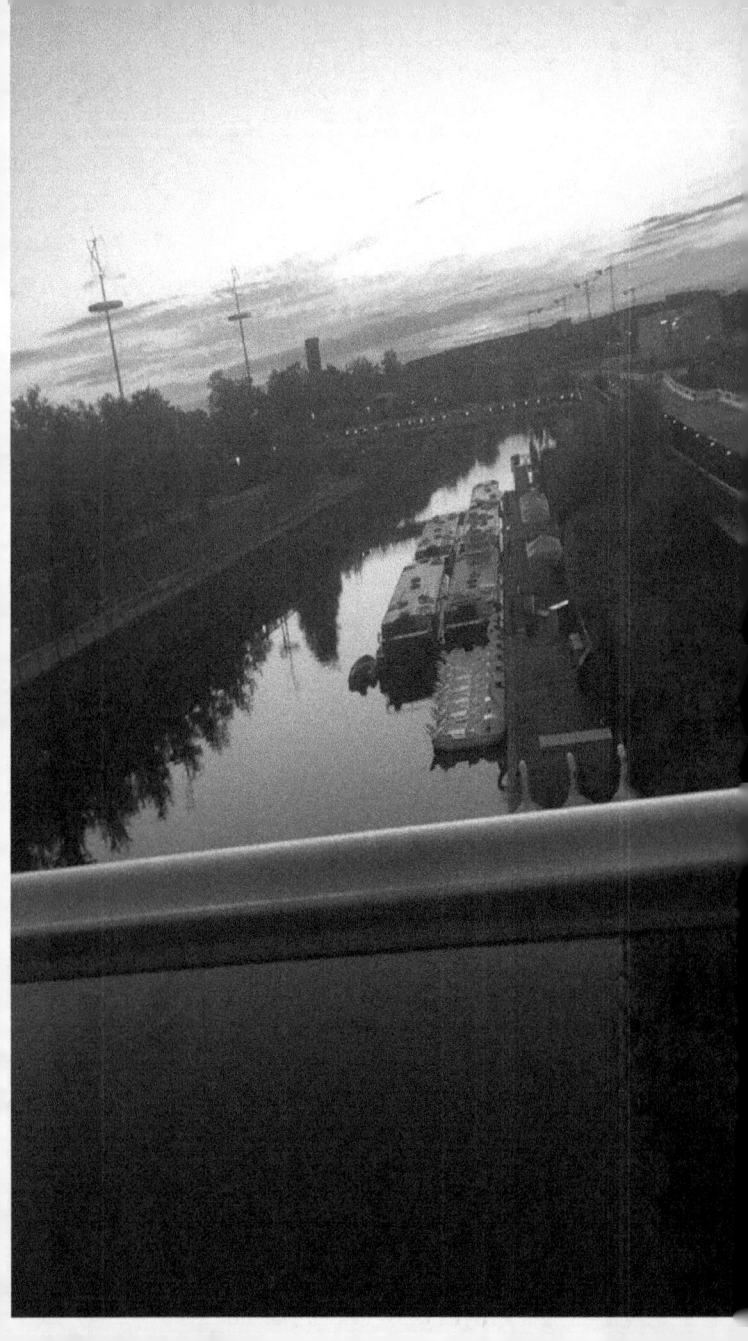

Wrong direction

I feel like I'm living a life full of lies,
like this is who I want to be, but is it,
this is who I love but is he, I'm lost
and have no direction, so I'm directing
myself somewhere I actually want to
be.

Yeah, I know

I know my life is not meaningless but as far as I can see it is, as I'm sitting here yearning to the world to tell me what path to take all I hear is silence, vibrating silence, the sound of the wind hitting the leaves, the sound of cars racing into the distances, sounds which are so familiar where I have grown to mask the sound of hearing them.

Darkness overpowers my light

So many emotions in one place, it's hard for me to control, they all want to be seen and heard but only one is seeing the light of day. So, I try to hide it away by staying away.

Nothing 'seems' to help

I try to buy my pain away,
but nothing objective makes
me feel any better, I could
be rich and still feel the
same depression and lonely
like my life is pointless and
I'm doing nothing to
contribute to society.

A burden who hangs around
and does nothing all day
because she's feeling a
sense of hurt and pain and
can't escape her feels, she's
lost in a tunnel that has no
ending.

The pain awaits

I felt the depression coming
on and consciously I knew
there was nothing I could
do about it and knew that
it would have consumed
me in a blink of an eye.

This feeling

Shivers up and down my skin when I breath in and out I feel the circulation of blood around my body, and my heart beating out my chest; my eyes seem to water and I don't know why, what is this? the world is suffocating me from both sides.

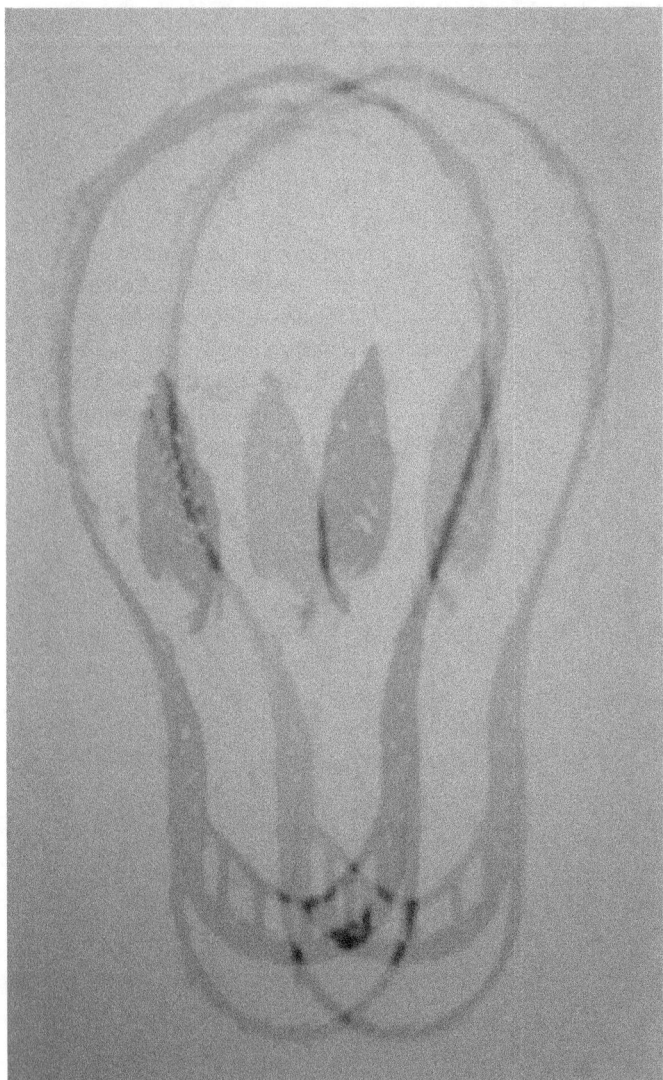

What control do I have?

A demon torments her mind, it tells her what to do, how to feel, what to say and how to live, she so lonely but can't do anything to help herself this demon is depression, and depression is a bitch.

Nowhere to hide

Like a thief in the night it
strikes again, unaware,
unprepared to feel its
draft.

I'm afraid of what's to
Come, unaware I'm left in
the dust not knowing
what's coming next,

how I'm going to feel and
what's the result going to
be.

I'm afraid of it all, I'm
afraid of myself but most
importantly I'm afraid of
this world.

I don't own me

She feels like she's
suffocating in her own
body, being eating alive like
there's a monster inside
her, she's being tormented
by her thoughts and
tormented by her
mind.

It's hard to see

As I walk down the colourless
streets I see the eyes of the
wicked and the eyes of soulless
beings, they seem to hide in plain
sight, so we don't see,

they're venomous creatures who
seek to poison the lives of living
beings.

Life isn't nothing but a curse

The amount of pain I have is
unbearable, how am I to go on
when all this pain consumes me
and is controlling my life,

I'm watching myself from the
inside out and it's unbearable
to see.

Left to my thoughts

Most times I just want to be left
alone, left to my own consciousness,
left to my own thoughts, but most
times it's the thoughts that lead on
the depression which puts me in a
state of contemplation.

Your more than what you think

She knows what she's doing is
wrong, but she doesn't care,
she's the keeper of her own
body but doesn't control her
mind, she's the keeper of
her own heart but
doesn't control
her emotions.

She's like a puzzle
that can't be solved.
A jigsaw which is
unbearable, she hates
herself and she says
it all the time,

she doesn't care
if she dies or not in fact
she would prefer to die.

My life is looking useless
and it's a waste of time
so why be alive when
I could just die.

How am I to be?

how am I to
speak my truth
when they don't
want to hear it.

How am I to be
me, in this world
when nothing is
accepted, my
opinion, my
views will get
looked across
because of my
age, my skin or
my gender,

so, tell me how
am I to be me in
this world when
nothing is
accepted.

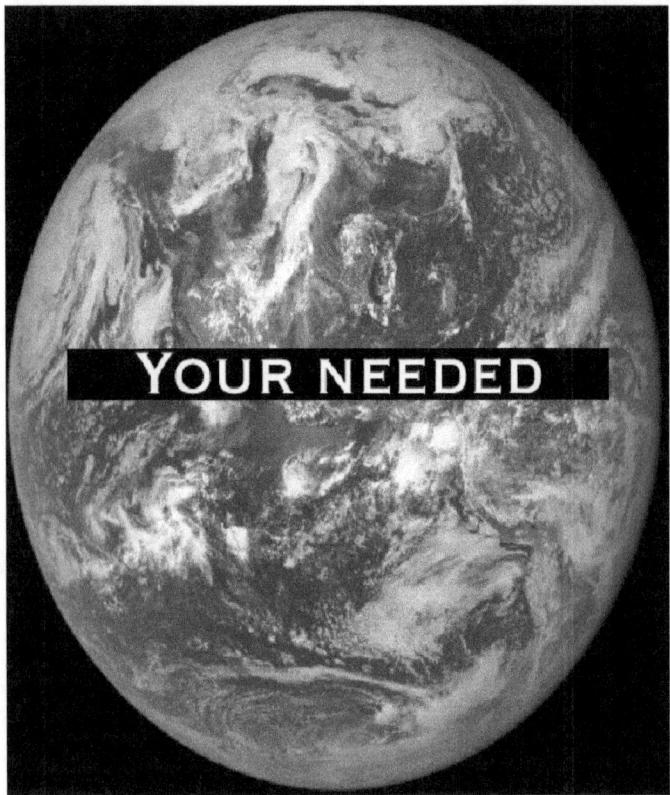
YOUR NEEDED

......

Her eyes told a story when I looked
into it. So soft, so gentle, so wise
beyond her years, she's experienced
things a young girl should never. Yet
she battles through because she's
more than the pain she holds.

My reflection lying to me

As she stares at herself in the mirror she's suffocating from her life and drowning in her own pain, she doesn't want to keep pushing she's tired and wants it to be over "she says" as she stares at herself in the mirror and contemplate.

I'm just a black girl....

I want to escape this cruel world; I want to escape my body I want to escape my soul. To change my appearance is nothing, but to change my feeling is hope, being me is not easy I'm a black girl living a life of cruel intentions and false hope.

Do they even care, or unaware

So many people around me but
I'm far from close to anyone, I'm
like the elephant in the room but
no one knows I'm there, except
for myself,

I'm unaware of their unawareness,
I'm thinking they don't care, when
really, they have no idea.

Until then

Just because you don't yet
know your purpose doesn't
mean you don't have one.

Is what it is

She feels like she's living a lie, living
a life which wasn't meant for her,
and forsaking who she's meant to
be;

she wakes up every day with the
same thought... this shit again and
put the covers back over her head
and hope for a change once again.

Misunderstood

They tell her to cheer up
like feeling sad is something
she's choosing to feel
something she can control.

Patiently waiting

Like the
darkness it
comes to me,

I'm aware of it
but I never see it
coming.

It creeps up on
me like the
spiders under
my bed,

it whispers in
my ear then
takes my mind
on a trip,

There's no
escaping
because it has
my mind under
its control

so, there's
nothing for

me to do but

patiently wait
until it lets me
go.

She tells me

She tells me that she's trapped in
her body and has no control over
what she thinks and does, she
tells me she feels like a passenger
in her own body wondering
around the empty hall's ways of
her mind.

She wants to escape but
she doesn't know how.
She's depressed all the time
she tells me and has thoughts
about dying, her anxiety gets
the best of her sometimes
which causes her to drift away
into a place that is dark
and tormented.

She tells me she feels empty
inside, and that her soul is hurting
and calling for help she has no
idea who she is or what's she's
meant to be so what's the point in
living,

She lets me know she's going to
take her own life, I tell her why,

she looks me in my eyes and tells
me life would be so much better
if I'm dead I wouldn't have to
worry about anything,

I'll be free, I'll be free from the
thoughts that haunt my dreams
free of the hatred In The world
just free from everything.

I tell her life is beautiful, magical,
And just because life is painful now
Doesn't mean it doesn't get better
so just wait and thank me later.

We Are All Beautiful, no matter our features

Don't hate yourself

It's my own kind that tires me down
and criticizes me for the same
features they have.

It's my own kind that's calls me ugly
and puts me down and comes for me
for me being me.

It's my own kind that tells me I should
hate my natural hair.

It's my own kind that tells me my skin
is disgusting and that they'll never
date a dark skin girl like me.

"It's my own kind"!!!!!!
That tells me this.... (Change)

Instead of looking down on each
other, let us up lift and show love to
one another because we all came
from being the minority and at the
end of the day, we are all brothers
and sisters who went through the
same pain.

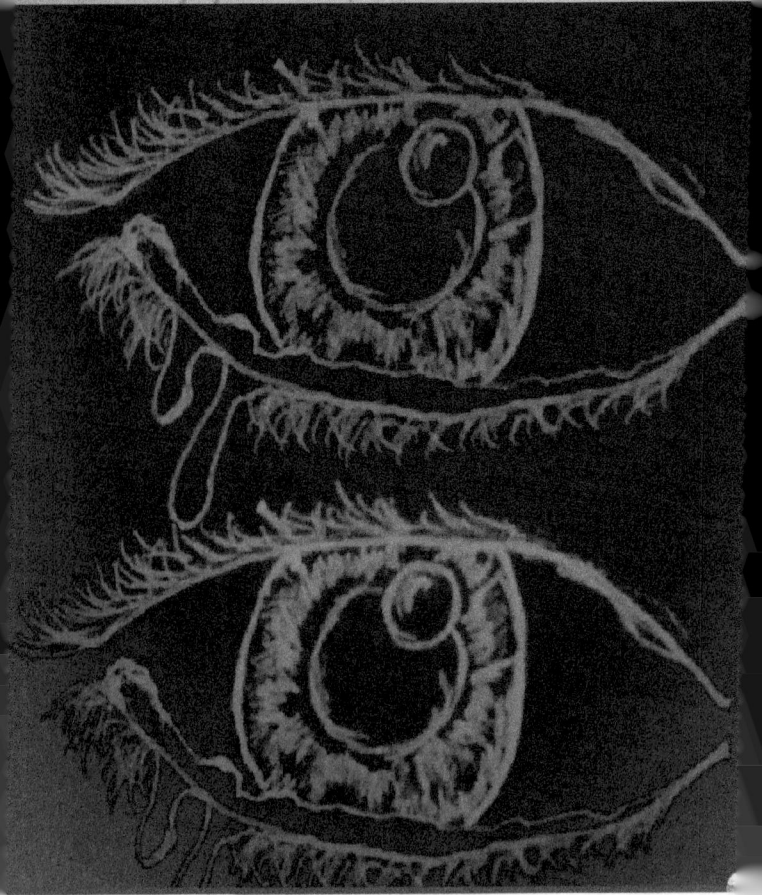

No need to hide it

I see the pain your trying to hide
inside, you keep it deep in your chest
hidden behind the lies you tell to
cover it up.

It comes out in the night when no
one's around and loneliness bites, it
becomes your body and takes over
your mind. Your paralyzed and have
no option but to watch yourself
become consumed from the inside.

Wise words

"She told me what's the point of
living if all she endures is pain in a
life with no happiness"

To reach the peak of true happiness
a person may have to walk over rocks
and stones and through a blizzard of dust,
where others walk over roses, everyone's
journey is different, but all that matters
is that you get there.

Graceful

I'm laying on a bed of roses
staring up at flowers of all
kinds, it's dark and the
moon is the biggest it's ever
been, so close I could
almost touch it,

I feel more alive than when I
was alive, a feeling that I
never felt a day in my life.

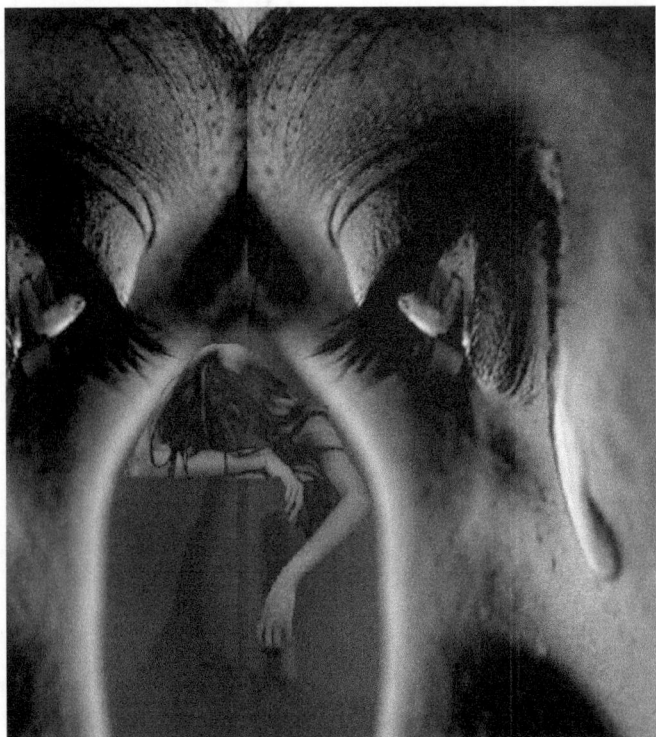

The day is near

The pain in her eyes is noticeable, I
know she's hurting, and I can see it in
her face she despises the fuck out of
herself and I can't wait until the day
she finds her smile.

We are not your enemy

You down grade us and are spitting in our faces'
when you deny us access, when it's your own
people committing these terrorist acts your
own people killing dozens, you brought us in
when you needed your houses to be built, your
crops to be harvested, your children to be
looked after and your food to be cooked. Now
you want to kick us out and deny us entrance
into something we built.

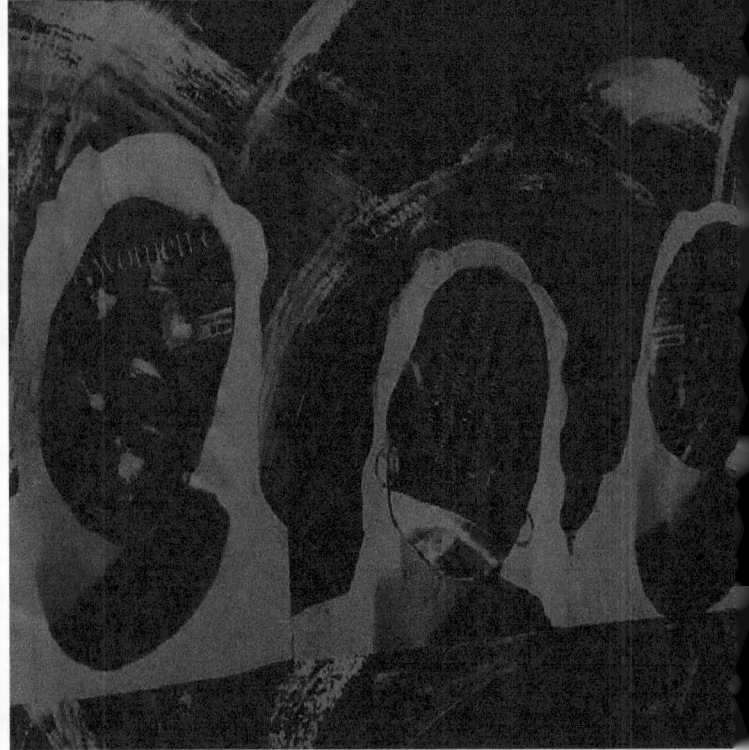

Is what it is

They talk behind my back like I don't
hear their whispers, they laugh in my
face like I don't know the truth, they
smile at me and concede in me with
their truths, meanwhile talk about me
when I leave the room.

Fake friends were fake from the start,
so don't make it hard to let them go if
they deceive your heart.

Not where I want to be

I walk down the street and I feel
the stares, I like to stand out but
sometimes I just want to dissolve
into the air.

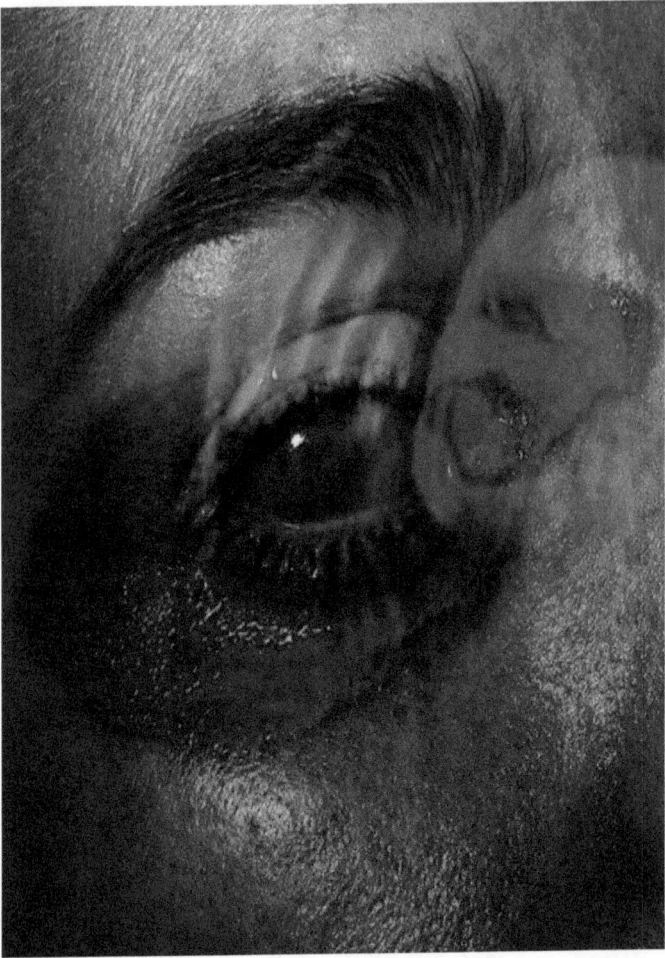

I thought I needed you

I need you but I'm scared of your love, you say you love me but turn around and abuse my trust, and say it's because I love you so much

You see I need you, but I'm scared of your love, you turn around and physically abuse me, and say once again it's because I love you so much.

Sometimes

Sometimes I wish I could live in
my dreams and be safe from the
world and safe from my feelings,
Free to walk around feeling like
this is where I'm meant to be,
this is the space I need.

Keep hiding behind your lies

How am I to trust in you when all you do is lie, I give you a chance to tell the truth, but all you do is tell me lies; I roll my eyes and walk away, and you sit there with a smile.

I need to let you go

It's hard for me to let you go because I still need you, it's hard to wrap my head around that your actually gone and there's no seeing you. I see you in my dreams but wake up and then reality hits and your nowhere to be seen.

Are you ready for the blame?

He hates himself he thinks he's
ugly but really, he's not however,
people tell him that, so he
believes them.

he thinks that's he worthless and
life is pointless as people tell him
that he's nothing, you see he's
been through a lot and no one
sees it, but there's only an
amount that someone can
take before they say, fuck this,
and does it.

Bonus
Poems

What can I say?

The pain I'm feeling is more Than physically, the world hasn't changed much since the days of horror towards minorities.

Who can I trust?

We're friends but you talk behind my
back, it's hard for you to be honest
with your feelings and despise me
because I'm so open and self-
expressed. Or maybe you're just
a bad person.

No exposure

The greatest freedom you
can feel, is waking up in the
morning and having
nowhere to be.

Pointless

I try not to stress when I
can't control a situation,
why stress if there's nothing
you can do. It's pointless.

Stop holding your pain

Your scared to show your truth, so
you suffer in silent, your scared of
the judgement so you hide behind your
alter egos. You feel it grow deep inside
you, but you avoid confrontation and
stay away hoping it will slowly fade into
the distance.

Lying is easy

Just because they say they love you
doesn't mean they care for you.

Just a little note

I need you more than I ever
needed anyone, you taught me
how to love myself, and that life
was more than which I thought it
was.

You taught me about the stars in
the night sky, the sun and its heat,
the river and its flow and why my
heart beats.

Speak your truth

Don't make it hard for you to open
your mouth and speak your truth
even if no one's listening. You are
your biggest fan.

Just Believe

everyday feels like torture every day I
wake up and have to force myself to do
something productive with my time
rather than laying in my bed wishing
for no light, everyday may be a struggle
but believe in the light.

Where am I

I'm lying in my bed and I'm alive,
yet I feel I'm gone from my body,
physically I'm here, spiritual I've gone
and disappeared, but my minds stuck
here with no way to escape, therefore
forced to endure the pains that comes
with living.

Trust me it is

Those days were the worst days
of my life I can't believe I went
through that and survived all the
lies or the hurt all the words that
were said. Which shows that your
stronger than any of the rest.

Locked in

Stop dwelling on the what
could have been and start
focusing on what's going to
be.

I shouldn't need you to make me happy

I'm reliant on you to make
me happy and forsaking true
happiness of oneself, you have
the control over me whether it
be good or bad, and I don't care
what you do with it.

All I needed

As I gaze out into the settling ocean, I feel all my worries and problems disappear, I feel a sense of release from my heart and the chains being dropped from my soul. Free at last.

We're all beautiful and divine

You're so beautiful, your soul and
your spirit. Your body and your mind.
You know I love you and don't think
I'm lying, because I say it all the time,
I let you know that your beautiful in the
mornings and your beautiful in night.

Stay strong it's okay

You're so strong, I know you've been
through a lot and I can see it, your
hiding behind your scars and trying to
conceal it.

You don't want to be vulnerable
because that means expressing your
feelings, and you're not ready for that
and it's okay.

It'll get better

just because your lonely,
don't lower yourself to
people who aren't worth
your time.

Confusing

It's hard for me to hate you,
because I love you so, it's
hard for me to love you
because your hard to love.

You're the greatest

You're as great as you want to be,
there's no stopping you but yourself
so, stop stopping yourself because
your greater than you think.

Love you first

Learning to love yourself is harder
than loving someone
else, remember that.